HEALTHY HOMES
Where Healthy Kids Grow
By
Singing… Praying… Affirming

HEALTHY HOMES

Where Healthy Kids Grow

By

Singing... Praying... Affirming

**HEALTHY HOMES: INSTRUCT...
ENCOURAGE... SUPPORT... HEAL**

Allan G. Hedberg, Ph.D.
Clinical Psychologist
And
Family Counselor

Copyright © 2025 by Allan G. Hedberg, Ph.D.

ISBN: 979-8-89465-103-3 (sc)
ISBN: 979-8-89465-104-0 (e)

All rights reserved. No part of this publication may be reproduced, distributed, or transmitted in any form or by any means, including photocopying, recording, or other electronic or mechanical methods, without the prior written permission of the author, except in the case of brief quotations embodied in critical reviews and certain other noncommercial uses permitted by copyright law.

Printed in the United States of America.

Integrity Publishing
39343 Harbor Hills Blvd Lady Lake,
FL 32159

www.integrity-publishing.com

*God, I will sing a new song for you;
I will play on a ten-stringed harp for you.*

David

DEDICATION

I lovingly dedicate this book to my eight very
special grandchildren and their parents . . .
The Careys: Amanda and Micah
The Hultbergs: Linnea, Johanna, David, and Birgitta
The Hedbergs: Charis and Elias

ACKNOWLEDGEMENTS

Renee Slaybeck – for her research assistance
Carolyn Linn – for her editing assistance
My wife, Bernice – for her encouragement and idea exchange
Dr. MacMannis – for his inspiration and example
Birger Gossner - for his contribution of Swedish prayers
My mother – for exposing me to all these songs and more as a child
Mrs. Dunn – for being my most impactful
teacher in elementary school. We even
sang songs during her English class

CONTENTS

Preface xv

PART I: Songs with Lessons in Personal Acceptance, Strength and Self-Confidence. 1
- Oh, Be Careful Little Eyes What You See 2
- Wise Man and The Foolish Man. 4
- I Love the Mountains 6
- Onward, Christian Soldiers. 8
- When the Saints Go Marching In. 10
- I Shall Not Be Moved 11
- I've Got Peace Like A River. 13
- Rocka My Soul 15
- Deep and Wide. 16
- Who Built the Ark?. 17

PART II: Songs with Lessons in Interpersonal Effectiveness 19
- Jesus Loves the Little Children 20
- The Birdies in the Treetops. 22
- Clap Your Hands 23
- This Little Light of Mine 25
- Stand Up, Stand Up, for Jesus. 27
- Joshua Fought the Battle of Jericho 29
- Praise Him 31
- Go Tell It On The Mountain 33
- I'm in the Lord's Army 35

PART III: Songs With Lessons of Healthy Living 37
- Standing In the Need of prayer 38
- Row, Row, Row Your Boat 40
- Down in My Heart................................42
- I've Got Peace Like a River 44
- Whisper a Prayer 46
- His Banner Over Me is Love.......................48
- Jesus Loves the Little Ones 50
- He's Got the Whole World in His Hands 52
- Climb, Climb Up Sunshine Mountain 54
- What a Friend We Have In Jesus....................56

PART IV: Lessons in Personal Faith 57
- Jesus Loves Me 58
- Old Time Religion 60
- Praise God from Whom All Blessings Flow..........62
- Do Lord 64
- Oh, How I Love Jesus.............................66
- Oh, Happy Day 68

PART V: THE PRAYERS OF CHILDREN 70
- Bedtime Prayer 71
- Meal Time Prayer.................................72
- Table Prayer 73
- Table Time Prayer................................75
- The Lord's Prayer 76
- The Psalm.......................................78
- God, Who Holds the Children Dear................79
- A Goodnight Prayer 80
- Good Night, Mr. Moon 81
- Thank You God for the Gentle Rain................82
- God Teach Me To Love My Family and Friends 83
- A Daily Prayer for Focus 84

PART VI: Affirmations For Children 85
- Affirmations For Children........................86

APPENDIX 89
- Advice for Parents and Youth Leaders 89
- The Personal Impact of Music on Children...........90
- Competent Kids: Why Some Are and Some Are Not?...92
- Books by Dr. Hedberg for Kids and Their Parents 94
- Media Aps for Singing Kids 95
- References 96

PREFACE

I recall my mother introducing me to instrumental music through the use of a 33 1/3 record of *Rusty in Orchestraville*. By listening, I got the full breadth of instruments and the appreciation of musical scores. Later, in college, I took a course in music appreciation, which opened my mind to classical music.

As we now consider introducing children to the psychological meaning within children's choruses, not only will they appreciate music and its message, but it will also help kids live life fuller and more meaningful lives. Again, every chorus carries both a message and a meta-message. Both are valid and important.

Psychological messages for personal growth are embedded in songs and choruses' children sing on Sunday and often hum to themselves during the week.

Every child who ever attended a Sunday School, summer camp, or Daily Vacation Bible School sung songs and choruses with a clear religious emphasis and personal meaning. They were sung with much gusto. Indeed, happy kids sang them loudly. Singing time was always a happy time for kids…and for adults, too.

The songs sung at these events had a particular purpose and a message for a child's spiritual growth. They also had an underlying message of a psychological nature designed to bring about a child's personal growth. What often happened, unfortunately, was that emphasis was placed on the spiritual message but the psychological message was neglected or overlooked.

In this volume, I am purposefully refocusing our attention on the psychological messages within these children's choruses and songs.

Both messages are important, not one more than the other. One for personal faith development and the other for personal and interpersonal growth.

When children sing and meditate on purpose-driven and age-appropriate songs, character is built. Social skills are likewise established, and emotional skills are affirmed. A recent survey found that 60% of boys who pray feel calm and peaceful.

There are several common themes found in children's choruses. These include:

- Songs Calm
- Songs Enrich
- Songs Teach
- Songs Connect
- Songs Encourage
- Songs Stimulate
- Songs Direct
- Songs Motivate

By reflecting on and meditating on the lyrics of choruses, children are guided in developing friendship, sharing information, living through experiences, enhancing communication skills, expressing gratitude, practicing kindness, fostering positive thinking, andliving with hope.

Parents, youth leaders, teachers, grandparents, and older siblings are encouraged to select a song and then sing them together with a child or children. Thus, providing a positive social atmosphere, a positive interpersonal sharing experience, and to focus a child's attention and state of learning on positive thinking and the development of positive traits of behavior.

Choruses have similar impacts to those of teaching pride. All choruses deserve our attention and thoughtful reflection. There is a lesson underneath each chorus for purposes of personal growth, just like heroes do for us. They both teach, encourage, support, direct, and instruct.

One might even imagine life without choruses and songs. In such situations, the trepidations in the life of a child cripples, impairs, weakens, and leaves a child without direction, support, and encouragement.

Furthermore, life is rich with heroes. Likewise, life is rich with songs and choruses along with the messages contained therein. I invite you to sing them, learn them, and be encouraged, strengthened, and enriched by them every day.

Allan G. Hedberg, Ph.D.

PART I

Songs with Lessons in Personal Acceptance, Strength and Self-Confidence

Many songs and choruses carry messages of personal acceptance, strength, and self-confidence. Through singing of songs and choruses, children are encouraged to focus on such themes. By singing these songs, children learn to absorb the message of personal acceptance, strength and self-confidence. Repetitive singing is a basic learning tool and helpful memorization strategy that enriches their daily life experiences.

Children with personal acceptance, strength, and self-confidence thrive. They tend to love life fully, take risks, and benefit from new learning experiences. They blossom from such experiences. They are sought out as budding leaders. Leaders are those who develop personal strength and confidence from their participation in a wide variety of life experiences, including music. As they grow older, they live life more fully. It is through these life experiences and the singing of songs and choruses that they learn the basic leadership skills of personal acceptance, confidence and strength.

By singing the songs in this section, kids are encouraged and guided in the process of building personal strength and self-confidence. Parents and teachers are urged to utilize these songs frequently, providing helpful guidance to ensure children understand and apply the messages in their daily lives.

Kids are Curious and Need Guidance in Exploring Their World...

> ### OH, BE CAREFUL LITTLE EYES WHAT YOU SEE
>
> Oh, be careful, little eyes what you see.
> Oh, be careful. little eyes what you see.
> There's a Father up above looking down in tender love.
> Oh, be careful, little eyes, what you see.
> Oh, be careful, little ears, what you hear.
> Oh, be careful, little ears, what you hear.
> There's a Father up above looking down in tender love,
> Oh, be careful, little ears, what you hear.
> Oh, be careful, little tongue, what you say,
> Oh, be careful, little tongue, what you say,
> There's a Father up above looking down in tender love,
> Oh, be careful, little tongue, what you say.

Curious kids are generally smart kids. They seek out new information and new experiences. They like to discover new things and ideas. It's fun to be around such kids, they are, in a sense, "little teachers" in disguise.

It is true. All of our senses are also subject to upsetting and hurtful experiences. Being exposed to trauma and other painful events are a few examples. These events may come into our lives unexpectedly, and some we expose ourselves to through the way we live. We all need to be alert and avoid the distressing experiences so prevalent in todays' world.

Hence, it's important for children to be taught to be careful about what they see, hear, do, and say. It is easy for children to unwittingly become involved in situations where they could be hurt physically and/or emotionally.

We must learn to be cautious but still maintain our curiousity. We also need to learn to moderate and manage our curiosity. Self-confident people avoid embarrassing others or creating harm for others or for themselves, for that matter.

~~~~~~~~~~

LESSON #1 – Discuss the importance of our eyes and ears and their role in allowing social influences to impact us.

LESSON #2 – Discuss how to avoid being exposure to upsetting experiences and various types of influences that may not be in our best interest.

THE POINT - Self-control and management of all our senses are vital for personal acceptance, strength, and confidence.

Kids Need Help to Learn How to Make Good Decisions...

WISE MAN AND THE FOOLISH MAN

The wise man built his house upon the rock (3x)
And the rains came tumbling' down.

The rains came down and the floods came up, (3x)
And the house on the rock stood firm.

The foolish man built his house upon the sand, (3x)
And the rains came tumbling' down.

The rains came down and the floods came up, (3x)
And the house on the sand went SMASH!

This catchy little song tells us about the qualities of those who are wise. Wise men make good decisions. They live a life of respect and live a life of respect. They respect others and expect to be treated with respect in return. A sign of wisdom is a consistent pattern of sound decision making.

Wise men think ahead and determine how they will act in certain situations. They take their time when making decisions. They consult others for advice before making a decision. They carefully read and study the topic or issue being considered before deciding. When they decide, they do it with the knowledge and facts. When a decision is made, it is more likely to be a wise decision with a positive outcome because they did their homework.

On the other hand, people who are not wise or foolish do not think ahead or plan for the future. They are not careful or thoughtful. They do not consider the options or count the cost of the decision pending. They do not take their time in making a decision. Consequently, projects go unfinished, ideas are not fully explored, and opportunities slip away. Foolish individuals often find themselves left behind. Others avoid them, and they are often lonely. They are avoided by others. As a result, life events and opportunities that come their way often crash to the ground, "smash."

~~~~~~~~~~

LESSON #1 -Discuss examples of good and bad decision-making.

LESSON #2 – List the traits of good and bad decision-makers. Provide examples and discuss the consequences of good and bad decision making.

THE POINT - Strive to become a wise decision-maker and a leader among your peers.

Kids Love to Explore and Learn New Things...

> ### I LOVE THE MOUNTAINS
>
> I love the mountains, I love the rolling hills;
> I love the flowers, I love the daffodils;
> I love the fireside when all the lights are low;
> Boom-de-ah-da, Boom-de-ah-da,
> Boom-de-ah-da, Boom-de-ah-da, Boom!

Being curious and eager to learnnew thing about our earth, sky, and even about each other as people, is one of the most valuable skills we can develop. Learning something new is always a good thing to do. As someone once said, "A student is not someone who knows a subject matter, but someone who has the desire to know more."

The more we learn of our universe, the more we come to appreciate and love our world and its wonders. We learn not only through our daily experiences but also by being quiet, inquisitive, and thinking imaginatively.

What we love, we become. If we love nature, we will become like it. If we love the sounds of silence, we will become comfortable with quietness.

~~~~~~~~~~

LESSON #1 – What is good about nature? Why do we need it? How did it come about? Discuss our responsibility as stewards of nature.

LESSON #2 – What do children like about nature? How do they enjoy nature? How do they, along with their families take care of nature?

THE POINT - God created our world of nature for us to enjoy, protect, care for, nurture, and share with others.

Kids Need to Know They Have a Leader...

> ### ONWARD, CHRISTIAN SOLDIERS
>
> Onward, Christian soldiers,
> marching as to war,
> With the cross of Jesus,
> going on before!
> Christ, the royal Master,
> leads against the foe;
> Forward into battle,
> see His banner go!
>
> Refrain:
> Onward, Christian soldiers,
> marching as to war,
> With the cross of Jesus
> going on before!

Being part of a group that strives for success and living a life of achievement is very important to people of all ages. Whether we live a life of peace or of conflict, God is present to lead the way, support, guide, instruct, and protect us.

The issue we all face is decising who will be our leader and whom we will follow? What philosophy or way of life will we choose? Kids will be exposed to all kinds of ideas, choices, and opportunities in life. Various ways of life are always before us. We need to be wise, thoughtful, and considerate as we choose our leader, the person of influence, and the values we will follow.

~~~~~~~~~~

LESSON #1 – Discuss leadership. What is it? Can you give examples of leaders? Are you a leader?

LESSON #2 - Discuss followership. Are you a good follower? When is it wise to follow someone, and when might it be unwise?

THE POINT - To be a good leader, you must first be a good follower.

Kids Join Groups to Achieve Belongingness . . .

> # WHEN THE SAINTS GO MARCHING IN
>
> Oh, when the saints go marching in,
> Oh, when the saints go marching in,
> Dear Lord, I want to be in that number,
> When the saints go marching in.
>
> Oh, when we crown Him King of kings,
> When we crown Him King of kings,
> Dear Lord, I want to be in that number,
> Oh, when we crown Him King of kings.

Some people prefer to avoid crowds. Most, however, prefer to be where the people are and where the action is. Parties, celebrations and joyful events bring people of all ages together. Wether it's a birthday party, a graduation, or a wedding, coming together for any reason is often a time of joy and celebration.

~~~~~~~~~~

LESSON #1 - When is it important to be in the middle of a crowd and follow its direction? When might it not be a good idea?

LESSON #2 - There are times when it' best to avoid crowds and not follow where they are going. Explain and give examples.

THE POINT - Be where the action is, but use good judgement.

Kids Need Support to Stand Firm Against Stress...

I SHALL NOT BE MOVED

I shall not be, I shall not be moved, (2x)
Just like a tree that's planted by the water, I shall not be moved.

Glory Hallelujah! I shall not be moved, (2x)
Just like a tree that's planted by the water, I shall not be moved.

When my burden's heavy, I shall not be moved (2x)
Just like a tree that's planted by the water, I shall not be moved.

Oh, if my friends forsake me I shall not be moved (2x)
Just like a tree that's planted by the water, I shall not be moved.

As we grow and mature, we establish the values, morals, and lifestyle that will define us for the rest of our lives. When this process of development is complete, we need to be like a tree planted by the water- firmly rooted and able to withstand the stresses of daily life and the inevitable storms that come our way.

No matter what friends or others may do, we must stand firm in our own beliefs and faith. Always be like a tree. It cannot be moved once established. We are to capitalize all our daily experiences and become mature and strong. Remember, it is not what happens to us, but how we respond to challenges that determine our strength. We grow strong accordingly.

~~~~~~~~~

LESSON #1 – What helps you stand firm when other kids try to pressure you into doing something you do not want to, or know you shouldn't do?

LESSON #2 – Describe a tree that is deeply rooted in soil and cannot be moved. How does this symbolize the kind of person you want to be?

THE POINT - Be a person of strong character, with clear values, attitudes, and behaviors that others notice and respect.

Kids need to bring peace into their lives . . .

I'VE GOT PEACE LIKE A RIVER

I've got peace like a river,
I've got peace like a river,
I've got peace like a river in my soul.(2x)

I've got love like an ocean,
I've got love like an ocean,
I've got love like an ocean in my soul. (2x)

I've got joy like a fountain,
I've got joy like a fountain,
I've got joy like a fountain in my soul. (2x)

I've got peace, love and joy like a river,
I've got peace, love and joy like a river,
I've got peace, love and joy like a river in my soul (2x)

Peace is an important experience worth pursuing. Once achieved, it is something worth protecting. A phrase to remember is, "Don't let anyone take your peace away." Peace comes from persistence. It often comes with a price.

We dream of peace. We speak of it as if we can hold it in our hands. We admire it in others. We write about it and even sing about it. Peace is indefinable, but we know it when we feel it.

~~~~~~~~~~

LESSON #1 – What is peace? How does a river serve as an image of peacefulness?

LESSON #2 – Why is an ocean often seen a peaceful image? When does it feel peaceful? How can we create a sense of peace though our imagination?

THE POINT - When we learn to use our imaginations, we can create a sense of peace and calm within ourselves when needed. Let us protect our peace and cultivate it from within.

Kids Need Guidance to Reach their Goals...

> ### ROCKA MY SOUL
>
> Rocka my soul in the bosom of Abraham, (3x)
> Oh, rocka my soul!
> So high you can't get over it, so low you can't get under it,
> So wide you can't get 'round it, you gotta go in at the door.

There are no shortcuts in life. There is a right way to do things and a wrong way. Always choose the right way when making decisions. Similarly, make the right choices when it comes to life style, behavior, selection of friends, and how you use your free time.

This spiritual has a long history, dating back to the late 1800s. It has been a guiding light for many throughout the years. It offers hope and encouragement in tough times when freedom seemed distant. Finding the "door" was a never ending pursuit to escape from bondage and the control of others. It is the same today as so many try to escape from stress, trauma and abuse. When life become overwhelming and seems impossible, there is always a "door." Just find it and walk through it.

~~~~~~~~~

LESSON #1 – Give examples of how shortcuts tend to lead to more trouble.

LESSON #2 – In life, do it the right way. Go through the door.

THE POINT - We all need comfort and guidance from those we love, along with their good advice and wisdom.

Kids Love to Sing and Feel Energized . . .

> # DEEP AND WIDE
>
> Deep and wide, deep and wide,
> There's a fountain flowing deep and wide. (2x)
>
> Wide and deep, wide and deep,
> There's a fountain flowing wide and deep. (2x)

Do you have a fountain of strength? A fountain of energy? A fountain of ideas and goals to pursue?

Ideas generate more ideas. Opportunities create more opportunities. Yes, we get more from where previous ideas and plans came from. One generates another, and so on.

~~~~~~~~~~

LESSON #1 – Where does our strength come from?

LESSON #2 – What is the source of your energy and strength?

THE POINT - Recognize that your energy and strength come from within you. Take not from your friends or social media, but if you do, give credit where it's due.

Kids Need Help and Protection from Stress...

> ### WHO BUILT THE ARK?
>
> Who built the ark? Noah! Noah!
>
> Who built the ark? Brother Noah built the ark.
>
> Old man Noah built the ark,
>
> He built it out of the gopher bark.
>
> He built it long, both wide and tall,
>
> With plenty of room for the large and small.
>
> In came the animals, two by two.
>
> Hippopotamus and kangaroo,
>
> In came the animals, three by three,
>
> Three big cats and three bumblebees.

We all face moments in life when the "storms of life" seem overwhelming. It is then we need a place of safety and protection. We also need to be with other people when we experience stress and hardship. The concept of an "Ark" symbolizes that safe place.

Sometimes, an ark is a physical place we can go for shelter. Other times, it represents people who provide care and safety. And sometimes, it is the ability within ourselves that we have to care for ourselves when times gets tough.

We all need an ark in our lives at some point. We also need people who can serve as an ark for us when we are in need.

~~~~~~~~~

LESSON #1 – Every person needs help from others. Discuss how we can all help each other.

LESSON #2 - Discuss the role of being a caretaker and protector, not just for others and for animals too.

THE POINT - Learn to be a helper when help is needed.

PART II

Songs with Lessons in Interpersonal Effectiveness

When we believe in God, we become part of the greater faith family. This family supports us as we grow in our faith while others grow in theirs. The family of God is vast and filled with opportunities to learn from one another.

As we grow in faith, we learn from each other. We share with each other. We help each other grow in the area of social skills. We do so in a multiple of ways. But it is mainly by example and watching how each other handles life events.

To be sure, interpersonal effectiveness is essential. It's a skill that helps us navigate the many different situations we encounter daily. Through song, we can learn and embrace the various relationship skills that will guide us in life.

Sing and learn the various relationship skills of life.

Kids are Good at Accepting Others . . .

> # JESUS LOVES THE LITTLE CHILDREN
>
> Jesus loves the little children
> All the children of the world
> Red and yellow, black and white
> They are precious in His sight
> Jesus loves the little children of the world.
>
> Jesus died for all the children
> all the children of the world
> Red and yellow, black and white
> They are precious in His sight
> Jesus died for all the children of the world
>
> Jesus loves the little children
> All the children of the world
> Red and yellow, black and white
> They are precious in His sight
>
> Jesus loves the little children of the world.

We live in a world filled with many different kinds of people. Many speak a different language. Many look different in color of skin. Many have different hair colors and types of hair style. And many people some from different background and hold diverse perspectives on life.

While we all see people differently, God sees all people the same. He created all of us with care and love.

Our task is focus on how we all are the same or similar rather than different. Also, we should think how we can help one another and learn from each other. Remember, being different, is not wrong or bad. It is an opportunity togrown, learn, and benefit from each other and by so doing we enrich our understanding of life and the world we live in.

~~~~~~~~~~~

LESSON #1 – How do you show love to others, regardless of their skin color?

LESSON #2 – Why should we get to know and love others, no matter their skin color?

THE POINT - We are all created by God and equal in value, and worthy of His blessings.

Kids Need Others to Be an Example of How to Up . . .

> ## THE BIRDIES IN THE TREETOPS
>
> The birdies in the treetops sing their song
> The angels chant the chorus all day long
> The flowers in the garden blend their hue,
> So why shouldn't I, why shouldn't you,
> Praise Him too?

Like the birds, we need to let others know where we are, what we are doing, and what we need. We need to speak out and have others join us. Then, we will not feel so alone or isolated. Birds show us the value of social communication skills. Singing out is like speaking out. Telling your story to others is a good way to become part of your social group, be noticed, and have a positive influence on those around us

~~~~~~~~~~

LESSON #1 – Who is a good example of strong communication skills, and why?

LESSON #2 – What makes communication effective? Discuss examples of good communication.

THE POINT - Good communication starts with good listening.

Kids Need to Learn How to Express Themselves . . .

CLAP YOUR HANDS

Clap, clap, clap your hands, clap your hands together (2x)

Clap a little harder now, clap along with me.

Clap a little Softer now, clap along with me.

Stamp, stamp, stamp your feet; stamp your feet together,

Nod, nod, not your head, nod your head together.

Shake, shake, shake your head, shake your head together.

There are many ways to express ourselves. Talking, singing, and even yodeling are a few examples. This song encourages us to clap our hands, stamp our feet, nod our heads, and shake our heads as form of social expression. We are encouraged to speak up, whether we are out with other people socially or when we are alone. In other words, we should not be the silent ones, but rather actively engage and become part of the social occasion. Bydoing so, we are appreciated and valued by others. We even feel better about ourselves.

~~~~~~~~~~

LESSON #1 – Practice each of the exercises in this song as examples of communication.

LESSON #2 – Practice putting words to each of the actions. Discuss how these actions are examples of communication.

THE POINT - Silence is not the answer; active communication leads to success.

Kids Need Help in Expressing Themselves...

THIS LITTLE LIGHT OF MINE

This little light of mine
I'm gonna let it shine
This little light of mine
I'm gonna let it shine
This little light of mine
I'm gonna let it shine
Let it shine, let it shine, let it shine

Hide it under a bushel; No!
I'm gonna let it shine!
Hide it under a bushel; No!
I'm gonna let it shine!
Let it shine, let it shine, let it shine

Don't let Satan blow it out
I'm gonna let it shine
Don't let Satan blow it out
I'm gonna let it shine
Let it shine, let it shine, let it shine

Let it shine till Jesus comes
I'm gonna let it shine
Let it shine till Jesus comes

I'm gonna let it shine
Let it shine, let it shine, let it shine

We may not think about it or believe it, but each of us has something valuable to share with others. We all have a story to tell, an experience to share, or an idea to propose. That is our "light" to shine for the benefit of others. We also benefit when we share our ideas with others.

Sometimes we blow out our own candle. Sometimes we let others blow out our candle. And sometimes, we just keep our light hidden, waiting for a "better" time to tell someone.

If you have an idea or experience to share, speak up. Share your thoughts. Encourage others to think, start discussions, and avoid staying silent.

~~~~~~~~~~

LESSON #1- We all have something to say or a story to tell. What's yours?

LESSON #2 – Commit to speaking up. Share what you think, and want others to know. Don't be passive; be assertive instead.

THE POINT - We all have a "light" to shine upon the world. Do it now. What is your message of light to the world?

Kids Need Help in Standing Up for What They Believe...

> ### STAND UP, STAND UP, FOR JESUS
>
> Stand up, stand up for Jesus,
> Ye soldiers of the Cross;
> Lift high His royal banner,
> It must not suffer loss.
> From victory unto victory
> His army shall He lead,
> Till every foe is vanquished,
> And Christ is Lord indeed.

For children to become effective adults, they must learn to be assertive in their communication skills. Children need to learn how to express their beliefs, feelings, ideas, or experiences that important to them.

Learning such skills comes from observing assertive communication in parents and other important adults. By watching these examples, children can imitate the desired behavior. Children need to be given permission to speak out, express themselves. Children need example and models to follow and imitate. Children need to be given opportunity to practice assertive communication skills. They need to be rewarded when they do speak out.

Becoming assertive is like becoming wise, skilled, and observant. Practice, practice, and practice is what it takes. Parents and teachers can create opportunities, and the child undergoes the practice. In time, the skill is learned and becomes part of their daily communication patterns. Parents are to reward their children when they do speak up. Encourage speaking out, not suppress their voices.

LESSON 1 – Do you find it easy or hard to stand up for something you believe in? How do you stand up for what is right? Can you share any examples?

LESSON #2 – Discuss a sample situation where it was important to stand up for what was right. How did you do it? How to get someone to help you do it even better?

THE POINT- Assertive communication skills are essential for being effective in all areas of your life. We need to express our faith, beliefs, ideas, feelings, and desires.

Kids Need Help in Standing up Against Opposition . . .

> ### JOSHUA FOUGHT THE BATTLE OF JERICHO
>
> Josua fought the battle of Jericho,
> Jericho, Jericho
> Joshua fought the battle of Jericho,
> And the walls came tumbling down!
>
> You may talk about your men of Gideon,
> You may talk about your men of Saul,
> But there's none like good old Joshua
> And the battle of Jericho!
>
> Joshua fought the battle of Jericho,
> Jericho, Jericho
> Joshua fought the battle of Jericho,
> And the walls came tumbling down!

We all have something in our live that we need to change. It could be a bad experience, negative thinking, a bad thought about someone, an undesirable habit, or even harmful thoughts about yourself. When we have these kinds of urges or thought patterns, we need to fight them off with the help of others and God.

As we grow older, it is possible to develop some bad habits that are not good for us. When we seek the help of others we can win the battle. Personal battles are not meant to be fought alone; we need to seek the help of people we trust in order to succeed.

~~~~~~~~~~~~

LESSON #1 – How does God tell you it is time to change your attitude, behavior or thoughts?

LESSON #2 - What habits do you need to change? How are you going to do it?

THE POINT - There are always people, forces, things, ideas, invitations, offers, and points of view we need to oppose, stand up against, and ultimately overcome.

Kids Need Praise from Others . . .

> # PRAISE HIM
>
> Praise Him, Him, all ye little children,
> God is love, God is love,
> Praise Him, Praise Him all ye little children
> God is love, God is love.

One of the important lessons to teach children is how to be grateful, honor others, and praise those who have performed a notable task. At such times, we need to appreciate what someone has done and the effort they put into it.

This chorus focuses on praising God as an example of the importance of praising others for what they have accomplished and for what they have done for you and others.

Children need to learn the language of praise, when to offer it, and to whom such praise-words are to be expressed. Parents serve as the primary teachers of praise expressions by setting an example. Parents also teach children the reason why it is proper to praise others at appropriate times.

Children who have learned to express praise are typically happy, socially appreciated, and valued by others. On the other hand, children who don't learn to express praise and do not do so are children who are often avoided, overlooked, and bypassed. They tend to be less happy.

Praising others is a primary skill. It is an essential verbal expression for children to be effective, appreciated, and included in the social circles of their peers.

LESSON #1 – Discuss why praise is a good thing. Give examples.

LESSON #2 – Teach how to engage in self-praise. When to do it? Why?

THE POINT - Be a person known for your attitude of happiness and ability to praise others.

Kids Enjoys Telling Stories and News . . .

> ## GO TELL IT ON THE MOUNTAIN
>
> Go tell it on the mountain
> Over the hills and everywhere
> Go tell it Go on the mountain
> That Jesus Christ is born

There are moments in our lives when we have important information to share or we've experienced a notable event or accomplishment that we want others to know about. Some kids need encouragement to tell their story. At times, they need permission to tell others. Or, they may need guidance in how to tell their stories to others. Most of all, they need the support of others when they do tell their stories to someone. Everyone wants their story to be accepted and not rejected of laughed at by others.

Children are often timid when it comes to sharing something important to them. As adults, we need to encourage them to tell what they think, what they experience, how they feel, and what they believe. As adults, we need to learn how to listen to our kids when they tell their stories.

As we grow and mature, we establish our values, morals, and lifestyle that will identify us for the rest of our lives. We need to be like a tree planted by the water that is firmly set and withstands the pressures of the wind, the rain, and the storms of life.

No matter whatothers do, we need to be firm in our own beliefs and faith. Always be like a tree. It cannot be moved once it's established.

~~~~~~~~~

LESSON #1 – Think of something about yourself that you'd like others to know.

LESSSON #2 – Talk about the difference in telling something to a friend, a family member, a stranger, or a new acquaintance.

THE POINT - Be a person who is proud of who you are and what you believe. Share it with confidence.

Kids Have a Deep Need to Belong . . .

> ### I'M IN THE LORD'S ARMY
>
> I may never march in the infantry
> Ride in the cavalry
> Shoot the artillery
> I may never zoom o'er the enemy,
> But I'm in the Lord's army.
>
> I'm in the Lord's army
> I'm in the Lord's army
> I may never march in the infantry
> Ride in the calvary
> Shoot the artillery
> I may never zoom o'er the enemy,
> But I'm in the Lord's army.

There are many important things in life. There are things we choose todo and things we choose not to do. It is like having and not having ceratin things. We all must come to the point where we decide what is truly important and necessary. We don't need everything, nor do we need to have all the things others have.

The questions we must continually ask ourselves s: What is really important? Is it more important to be busy with activities, or be part of a Faith or Belief system?

Should we follow the actions of our friends and peers, or should wefollow our faith in God?

~~~~~~~~~

LESSON #1 – Discuss what it feels like to belong and how it feels to be excluded and not belong.

LESSON #2 – What is God's army? Are you part of it?

THE POINT - What is most important about belonging?

PART III

Songs With Lessons of Healthy Living

It is important for children to live a healthy life. Healthy kids are happy, productive, and motivated. They have energy, purpose, goals, and friends. Their health gives them the power to stay focused and keep going.

Healthy kids often sing. They also hum, and create music of their own. Music is a good part of their life. Over time, healthy kids are appreciated and desired. They have many friends. They are appreciated and looked up to by others, especially their peers.

Kids Need a Touch, Hug, and a Reliable Connection...

> ## STANDING IN THE NEED OF PRAYER
>
> It's me, it's me, it's me O Lord
> Standin in the need of prayer
> It's me, it's me, it's O Lord
> Standin in the need of prayer
> Not my father, not my mother,
> But it's me, O Lord
> Standin in the need of prayer
> Not my sister, not my brother,
> But it's me, O Lord,
> Standin in the need of prayer

Children know when they are in a state of need. They know when they need attention, support, encouragement, a touch, a pat on the back, or just a hug. They also know deep within themselves when they need someone to pray with them. If these forms of support do not come naturally, kids will find ways to obtain it, even in ways that are inappropriate.

Children also have an innate sense of when they are loved, when someone is willing to listen to them, care for them, or willing to provide some form of assistance. They can tell when they are with someone who will not abandon them.

Ultimately, children know that their greatest need and their most important need can be and should be met by their parents. When parents fail, siblings fail, and friends fail, children need to know that there is one who will listen, care for them, and support them in their time of need. That person is God. He will be there to ease their anxietie. He will be there when life and relationships are uncertain and stressful. It is through prayer that one is assured, comforted, and affirmed.

~~~~~~~~~~

LESSON #1- Why is it a good thing to ask someone to pray for you?

LESSON #2 – How do you ask for prayer? Give examples.

THE POINT - There are times when we need the prayer support and encouragement of others. Don't hesitate to ask for it, even from God Himself.

Kids Generally Want Help When Undertaking Difficult Tasks ...

> # ROW, ROW, ROW YOUR BOAT
>
> Row, Row, Row your boat
> Gently, down the stream,
> Marily, Marily, Marily, Marily,
> Life is but a Dream.

Children need a time and place to decompress, unwind, and seek peace. Life can often be stressful. The demands of school, homelife, and peer-driven activities, often are too much and exhausting. Chronic stress is exhausting and debilitating for anyone. Kids gradually weaken from high levels of chronic stress – social stress, educational stress, family stress, physical stress, and especially peer-driven stress.

Time is needed to get away from the ongoing pressure of stress. A place is needed to destress. Activities are needed to change the pace of ongoing stress to a more even state of calmness.

This is where "rowing your boat" comes in. Every kid needs a "boat" to row. For some its walking, exercise, bike riding, swimming, singing, drumming, or dancing. Every kid has his own preferred way to relax and prepare to face the stresse of life another day.

~~~~~~~~~~

LESSON #1 – Give examples of taking on a task by yourself compared to taking on a task with someone else. What is the difference?

LESSON #2 – What does it mean to "row your boat ashore"?

THE POINT - Life is stressful, and we need to learn ways to manage it and seek help when necessary.

Some Kids Feel Depressed and Call Out for Help...

> ### DOWN IN MY HEART
>
> I have the joy, joy, joy, joy,
> Down in my heart, (where?)
> Down in my heart, (where?)
> Down in my heart!
> I have the joy, joy, joy, joy,
> Down in my heart, (where?)
> Down in my heart to stay!
>
> And I'm so happy, so very happy,
> I have the love of Jesus in my heart!
> And I'm so happy, so very happy,
> I have the love of Jesus in my heart!

One of the deepest and most sought after feeling in life is joy. With joy come peace. With joy comes comfort. With joy comes excitement. With joy comes happiness.

Joy doesn't come from things we buy or events in which we engage, or even the things we do with or for other people. Joy, ultimately, comes from a deep but subtle feeling within oneself – a feeling of being accepted, appreciated, and valued by those important to us.

In other words, when we feel valued and accepted, we experience joy. When we have inner peace, we feel joy. When we feel included, we feel joy.

LESSON #1 – Design an acronym for the word J O Y to reflect the inner peace of joy.

LESSON #2 – Discuss joy and happiness. Explain their similarities and differences.

THE POINT - Joy, peace, and happiness are acquired and learned behavior patterns. Each day, take note of when you experience these states of mind.

Kids Need a Peaceful Living Environment . . .

I'VE GOT PEACE LIKE A RIVER

I've got peace like a river
I've got peace like a river
I've got peace like a river in my soul
I've got peace like a river
I've got peace like a river
I've got peace like a river in my soul

Sitting by a meandering river is relaxing, peaceful, and calming. So are the melodic and rhythmic waves of an ocean. Such relaxing experiences bring about feelings of enjoyment, peace, solitude, and quietness. We all need moments and places to experience a special moment of peace. This is when we quiet our minds and calm our bodies.

When a child needs to calm down and find peace, it is time to use their imagination and imagine a river, a river flowing, or an ocean beach with stillness. Such scenes can create a mind-state of quietness and calmness. By quieting the mind through imagination, one quiets the body and the emotions.

To create such a mind-set of calmness and quietness, calm music can play a major role. By going to a quiet environment, such as a child's bedroom for a "Quiet -Time" and listen to music or sing a selected song could be just the right way to refocus one's attention to achieve calmness in the midst of a family storm or state of chaos.

Rivers have always represented a place pf peace, quietness, and relaxation. Use the image of a river to regulate your emotional and mental states.

The chorus, I've Got Peace Like A River, may be just the perfect combination for such a time as this. The principle is, "Change your mind-set, change your behavior, and change your social environment." Then you will create a better life pattern of behavior. Rivers represent peace, quietness, calmness, and stillness.

It is often said that we have love as big as an ocean for our children, our grandchildren. We also speak of the joy within us which springs out and spreads onto others as a fountain of water. This little idea reminds us that within us we have capability, we have potential, we have skill, we have feelings, and we have something to share with others, such as peace, love, and joy.

~~~~~~~~~~~

LESSON #1 – Discuss a time when you walked along a river or played in a river. What was the memory? Was it a joyful and peaceful time?

LESSON #2 – Discuss a river experience that you will never forget. Why was it so memorable?

THE POINT - Learn to use your imagination to envision a peaceful river and think how to let your mind focus on that peaceful river as if you were actually there in person.

Kids Need Regular Emotional "Tune-Ups"...

> ### WHISPER A PRAYER
>
> Whisper a prayer in the morning
> Whisper a prayer at noon,
> Whisper a prayer in the evening
> To keep your heart in tune.
>
> God answers prayer in the morning
> God answers prayer at noon,
> God answers prayer in the evening
> So, keep your heart in tune.

A daily calming experience is needed for children to balance the excitement of their day. Calmness helps to ease the daily restlessness and tensions that naturally occurs for children and their parents. At such times, we need to learn how to calm our minds, feelings, interpersonal relationships, bodies, and even our speech. Calming exercises allows us to relate to others better, focus on homework, sleep, and generally feel more at ease.

Using internal practices like meditation, reflection, and prayer are helpful ways to regulate emotions, feelings, and thoughts. Accordingly, we can also change our mind-set from agitation to calmness, from irritation to peace, and from hyperactivity to stillness.

To achieve calming skills, children needs to practice strategies of creating calmness, such as through the use of songs that create a state of calmness. The use of these types of songs needs to be encouraged daily and used at different times of the day. Emotional regulation results when such songs are sung, hummed, or even imagined. The living environment can be changed to achieve and instill a state of calmness. In so doing, relationships will flourish, families will thrive, and children will become happy kids. Who wouldn't want that?

~~~~~~~~~~~

LESSON #1 – Define whisper. What does it mean to whisper a prayer?

LESSON #2 – Raise your hand if you ever whispered a prayer. Was it helpful? Tell us the story if you would like to share.

THE POINT - Learn to live a quiet and peaceful life by saying a daily prayer or singing a song that promotes mindful quietness.

Kids Have a Deep Desire for Reassurance...

> # HIS BANNER OVER ME IS LOVE
>
> The Lord is mine and I am His
> His banner over me is love
> The Lord is mine and I am His
> His banner over me is love
> The Lord is mine and I am His
> His banner over me is love
> His banner over me is love!

To feel important and accepted gives us a sense of value. The banner that all children seek to have over them is the love of others, especially their family. It is through the love of the family that children come to know what it is like to be loved and how to love others. A banner is a protection, a shield of protection. The love of family is one major banner of love we all desire and need.

We learn to receive love. We learn how to give love to another. We discover the essence of what love really is. We learn to share love. We learn to love others as we receive love from others. We learn to interact in a loving manner. All aspects of love are learned. It all starts with being loved. It all is underscored by knowing that we have a banner of love over us and that banner is God's love as well as love of the family.

~~~~~~~~~

LESSON #1 – How do we learn to show love to others?

LESSON #2 – How do you know when someone loves you and that someone is protecting you?

THE POINT - Knowing that there is a protective shield of love over you is comforting. And it makes you feel valued and supported.

Even Small Kids Need to Know They are Loved...

> ### JESUS LOVES THE LITTLE ONES
>
> Jesus loves the little ones like me, me, me. Jesus loves the little ones like me, me, me. Little ones like me sat upon His knee. Jesus loves the little ones like me, me, me.
>
> Jesus loves the little ones like you, you, you. Jesus loves the little ones like you,
>
> you, you. Little ones like you, saves them thru and thru, Jesus loves the little ones like you, you, you.

Every child, from an early age, wants to be loved. They know they are being loved when it comes into their daily life experience. Comfort, kindness, and gentleness are the hallmarks of all loving relationships and in all loving environments. We are perfectly acceptable to God just the way we are.

We don't need to change who we are. We don't need to change our appearance. We are created perfectly as we are. Jesus loves us just like we are. The way we were created allows us to come into the presence of God and be accepted. We can also relate to our friends knowing that we are who we were meant to be.

~~~~~~~~~~~~

LESSON #1 – Ask how the love of their mother/father is expressed in daily family life.

LESSON #2 – How do we know we are loved? How do we show we love someone?

THE POINT - We are loved, even when we are small and may even feel unimportant.

Kids Need to Know They are Never Alone...

> ### HE'S GOT THE WHOLE WORLD IN HIS HANDS
>
> He's got the whole world in His hands,
> He's got the whole world in His hands,
> He's got the whole world in His hands,
> He's got the whole world in His hands.
> He's got the wind and the rain in His hands,
>
> He's got the wind and the rain in His hands,
> He's got the wind and the rain in His hands,
> He's got the whole world in His hands.
>
> He's got you and me, brother, in His hands
> He's got you and me, brother, in His hands
> He's got you and me, brother, in His hands
> He's got the whole world in His hands

One of the deepest and most painful emotions anyone can experience is the feeling of being abandoned, neglected, forgotten, or rejected. Such hurtful feelings are deep and can last a lifetime.

The opposite is what we seek. We want to be part of the life of others. We want to belong to others. We want to belong to a family. We want to belong to a circle of friends. We want to be where the action is. It is a good feeling to be wanted. It is a good feeling to be accepted. It is a good feeling to be included. It is a good feeling to be supportive, enriched, and protected.

It is in the hands of a loving, caring, and supportive person that we grow and become fully human.

~~~~~~~~~~~~~

LESSON #1 – Describe what it is like to be in someone's hands. What does that phrase make you feel?

LESSON #2 – The whole world? What does that mean? Does it include you?

THE POINT - Know you are protected and valued, never forgotten.

Kids Need Someone to Help them When Times are Tough...

CLIMB, CLIMB UP SUNSHINE MOUNTAIN

Climb, climb up sunshine mountain,
Heav'nly breezes blow.
Climb, climb up sunshine mountain,
Faces all aglow.
Turn, turn your back from doubting,
Looking to the sky;
Climb, climb up sunshine mountain
You and I.

This chorus was meant to remind us to focus our attention on Jesus as the one who is with us in all situations. It encourages us to excel and go forward rather than to doubt and withdraw.

There are many situations in life that seem like mountains to climb. It could be math, reading, or it may be a particular social skill or a particular athletic skill.

This song reminds us that we are not alone and that we can undertake difficult tasks, even impossible tasks. Even tasks which seem impossible can be accomplish when we have a support system that encourages us and will do things with us. This support could come from a parent, a best friend, a grandparent, a relative, a neighbor, a youth leader, or a pastor. The main thing is to understand that we are not alone and that we have people in our life who can help us through the tough things.

LESSON #1 – Who is your support person? How are you supported? Tell us about it.

LESSON #2 – Are you a support person for someone? Tell us about it.

THE POINT - Let someone help you when you need help; your turn to help someone else will come.

Kids Need to Have Many Friends . . .

> ### WHAT A FRIEND WE HAVE IN JESUS
>
> What a friend we have in Jesus;
> All our sins and grief he bears.
> What a privilege to carry
> Everything to God in prayer

Friendships are vital for fulfilling life and for building long-term relationships. With a friend, we are never alone. We all need the ongoing support of a trusted friend.

It is a privilege to be able to share and learn from another friend. Friends are

those who listen, support us, and give good advice when needed. Friends are always available and ready to act as needed.

We don't need many friends, but we do need a few who are reliable and truly special to us. Long-term friends are the most valuableof all.

~~~~~~~~~~

LESSON 1 - Talk about friendship and how important it is to have a variety of friends we can trust.

LESSON 2 – Talk about past experience with friends. Bad friends and good friends are both part of our life and need to be distinguished.

THE POINT - To make a friend you must first be friendly.

PART IV

Lessons in Personal Faith

When we believe in God, we become part of a faith family. This family helps us grow in our faith while we help others grow in their faith also. The family of God is a large family. There is a shared sense of belongingness.

As we grow in faith, we learn from each other. We share with each other. We help each other grow in the faith. There is a desire to help each other deepen our faith and understanding of God. There is a bond of oneness, togetherness.

Remember, we see people as being different; God sees all people the same as He created them.

Know They are Loved Deeply . . .

JESUS LOVES ME

Jesus loves me this I know,
for the Bible tells me so,
Little ones to him belong,
They are weak but He is strong.

Jesus loves me, He who died
Heaven's gate to open wide;
He will wash away my sin,
Let his little child come in

Jesus loves me, loves me still,
Though I'm very weak and ill;
From his shining throne on high
Comes to watch me where I lie

Jesus loves me, He will stay
Close beside me all the way.
Then his little child will take

Children need to know that they are loved and that they can live a life of confidence rooted on that love. No child should ever feel alone or be left behind. No matter what the situation or circumstance, we are never alone. Jesus is always with us and reminding us that we are loved and that we have value.

Confidence comes in knowing that you have friends and a support system. People around us offer encouragement, love and care.

When we feel love, we have the freedom to explore and be creative. We can invent and try new things. We can act with confidence and courage. This song assures us that there is always a foundation of love in our lives. Jesus is the first and the basic love of our life. Others follow in their expressions of love such as parents, grandparents, and friends.

~~~~~~~~~~~

LESSON #1 – How do we know someone loves us?

LESSON #2 – Why is it important to know someone loves us?

THE POINT - We learn to love others as we are loved.

Kids Need Encouraging Examples in Their Faith Journey...

> ## OLD TIME RELIGION
>
> Give me that old time religion,
> Give me that old time religion,
> Give me that old time religion,
>   It's good enough for me.
>
> It was good for Paul and Silas,
> It was good for Paul and Silas,
> It was good for Paul and Silas,
>   It's good enough for me. (Refrain)
>
> It was good for the Hebrew children,
> It was good for the Hebrew children,
> It was good for the Hebrew children,
>   It's good enough for me. (Refrain)
>
> It was good for our mothers,
> It was good for our mothers,
> It was good for our mothers,
>   It's good enough for me. (Refrain)
>
> Makes me love everybody,
> Makes me love everybody,
> Makes me love everybody;
>   It's good enough for me.

When we believe in God and put our trust in Him, we become part of a family of faith. The family of God is a large and inclusive family. This family helps us grow in our faith, just as we help others grow in their faith.

As we grow in faith, we learn from one another. We share with each other. We help each other live a life of faith. Thereby, we develop confidence in our faith and in our faith-based relationships. Living a life of faith is fostered by our relationships. We gain confidence and strength from each other when we share a common faith and develop that faith together as family and friends.

~~~~~~~~~~

LESSON #1 – Discuss the differences between religion and faith.

LESSON #2 – Discuss the advantages of having a faith similar to that of your parents, grandparents, and other extended family members and friends.

THE POINT - Religion is the external, behavioral, and formal manner by which we develop our understanding of faith. Spirituality is the way to live out and reflect our personal faith in God in all areas of life.

Kids have Trouble Believing in God as their "Higher Power"...

> ### PRAISE GOD FROM WHOM ALL BLESSINGS FLOW
>
> Praise God from whom all blessings flow
> Praise Him all creatures here below
> Praise Him above, ye heavenly host
> Praise Father, Son, and Holy Ghost

One important lesson to teach children is how to be grateful, honor others, and offer praise when someone has done something notable or appreciated by others. This chorus focuses on praise to God. It is an example of the importance of our praising others for what they have accomplished and what they do for you.

Children need to learn the words of praise, when to express those words, and to whom such words are to be expressed. Parents are the teachers of praise. Parents teach children when to praise others, how to praise others, and why to praise others.

Children who have learned to express praise are happy children, socially appreciated, and sought out by others. On the other hand, children who do not learn to praise are children who are often avoided, overlooked, and bypassed in social situations.

Praising others is a primary skill and essential verbal expression for building effective relationships, appreciation, and inclusion in social circles.

LESSON #1 – Tell us how you praised someone recently. How did it make you feel?

LESSON #2 – How do you know that others like to be praised and commended?

THE POINT - Children who learn to express praise to others are happy and appreciated.

Kids Need to be Affirmed and Reassured of not Being Forgotten...

> ### DO LORD
>
> Do Lord, oh, do Lord, oh, do remember me, Do Lord, oh, do Lord, oh, do remember me, Do Lord, oh, do Lord, oh do remember me, Look away beyond the blue.
>
> I've got a home in glory land that outshines the sun, I've got a home in glory land that outshines the sun, I've got a home in glory land that outshines the sun, Look away beyond the blue.
>
> Do Lord, oh, do Lord, oh, do remember me, Do Lord, oh, do Lord, oh, do remember me, Do Lord, oh, do Lord, oh do remember me, Look away beyond the blue.

We all have deep and intense feelings for the support, love, and care we receive from our parents. Likewise, we also feel they need for such reassurance from others also. The richer, truer, and purer the attention, acceptance, and the care from others, the better. We all stand in need of support, encouragement of companionship. It is like a basic need. When we are on the receiving end of such care, we become healthier and our personal growth and maturity develop.

On the other hand, one of the deepest feelings of hurt is associated with being forgotten, neglected, overlooked, or left behind. We all cry out for someone to notice us, remember us, include us. When we are included, we feel like we have a home, a place of comfort, and a place of honor.

Yes, we need to be remembered, but more importantly, we need to be celebrated for who we are and what we have accomplished, and what we contribute.

~~~~~~~~~~~~~~~

LESSON #1 – Being remembered by someone is a great experience. Discuss a time when you were remembered and how it made you feel.

LESSON #2 – No one wants to be forgotten, neglected, or overlooked. Discuss what it feels like to be forgotten. Remind them that God never forgets us.

THE POINT - Know you are remembered for who you are, neverforgotten, and never left behind.

Kids need to receive much love from others . . .

> ### OH, HOW I LOVE JESUS
>
> There is a name I love to hear,
> I love to sing its worth;
> It sounds like music in my ear,
> The sweetest name on earth.
>
> Oh, how I love Jesus,
> Oh, how I love Jesus,
> Oh, how I love Jesus,
> Because He first loved me.

Children thrive on being loved. It is one of the essential ingredients for positive personal growth. Being loved is the basis of learning how to love and how to express love to others. We naturally love deeply and strongly, those that love us.

Love messages come in many forms. Words expressed provide the affirmation and encouragement on which we thrive daily. Mutual companionship is another way to show others that they are appreciated and loved. The giving and receiving of gifts also communicate our love for someone.

~~~~~~~~~~

LESSSON #1 – How do you express your thanks when someone gives you a gift?

LESSON #2 – Think of all the ways you can express your appreciation to someone.

THE POINT - Being loved starts with the process of loving others first.

Kids desire to be happy . . .

OH, HAPPY DAY

Oh happy day (oh happy day)
Oh happy day (oh happy day)
When Jesus washed (when Jesus washed)
When Jesus washed (when Jesus washed)
When my Jesus washed (when Jesus washed)
Washed my sins away (oh happy day)
Oh happy day (oh happy day)

Oh happy day (oh happy day)
Oh happy day (oh happy day)
When Jesus washed (when Jesus washed)
When Jesus washed (when Jesus washed)
When Jesus washed (when Jesus washed)
He washed my sins away (oh happy day)
Oh happy day (oh happy day)

He taught me how (oh, He taught me how)
To wash (to wash, to wash)
Watch and pray (to watch and pray)
Watch and pray
And he taught me how to live rejoicing
Yes, He did (and live rejoicing)
Oh yeah, every, every day (every, every day)
I'm sayin' Every day!

Oh happy day, yeah (oh happy day)
Oh happy day (oh happy day)
When Jesus washed (when Jesus washed)
When Jesus washed (when Jesus washed)
When my Jesus washed (when Jesus washed)
My sins away (oh happy day)
Oh happy day.

Happiness is something every kid seeks. Our search for happiness is one of ourstrongest desires, driving many of the choices we make. Most of what we do is to gain a sense of happiness. Where we go, people with whom we associate, what we eat and drink, what we wear, and what we do for free time. Sometimes, we even take risks to find happiness.

True happiness, however, is found when one finds Jesus. That is when the scale of happiness is tipped in our favor. So, never stop the pursuit of genuine happiness.

~~~~~~~~~~

LESSON #1 – What makes you happy?

LESSON #2 – How do we feel when we are not happy?

THE POINT - Happy is the person (or child) who's God is the Lord.

PART VI

THE PRAYERS OF CHILDREN

Over the years, saying prayers with children has been a primary means of instilling faith in God.

Children's prayers have also serves as a tool for teaching them basic theology and Biblical Scripture.

Good night prayers, in particular, have been a comforting ritual, helping to calm children before bedtime and encouraging peaceful sleep.

Prayers have been a way to teach children the value and place of hope, faith and reliance on God, nurturing their spiritual development from an early age.

Kids need support and reassurance especially at bedtime . . .

BEDTIME PRAYER

Now I lay me down to sleep
I pray the Lord my Soul to keep.
If I should die before I wake,
I pray the Lord my Soul to take.

This is a prayer of support and reassurance. Kids need constant messages of support and reassurance from their parents. This prayer provides that comfort at bedtime. Bedtime is a time when kids often seek reassurance. Learning to place confidence in others is a fundamental skill acquired in childhood, which helps build strong relationships in adulthood.

LESSON #1 – Learn the prayer by repeating it regularly.

LESSON #2 – Discuss the prayer in detail adjusting to the child's age and understanding.

THE POINT - Meet a basic need of kids at bedtime – reassurance.

Kids need to learn to recognize the source of the good things in life . . .

MEAL TIME PRAYER

Come Lord Jesus,
Be our guest.
May all this food to us be blessed.
Amen

Sometimes a short and simple lesson can teachprofound ideas and life values. It starts by being tankful for the daily food and then goes on to teach the life lesson of being thankful for all things.

The lesson of welcoming others into your life and sharing expereinces with them is a basic life lesson of great value.

LESSON #1 – Learn the prayer.

LESSON #2 – Discuss the prayer and apply it to your child's life.

THE POINT - Always be thankful.

Kids need to be encouraged to be thankful and know how to learn from prayers . . .

TABLE PRAYER

In the name of Jesus to the table we go.
Bless, God, the food we receive.
And protect with your gentle hand
in grace our home and fatherland.

For food and drink you gave us here
praise be to you, O dear Lord.
All of us from that bread given
who gives eternal life.

This is an old Swedish prayer, recited at every meal in nearly every home in Sweden for many generations. It is a well-memorized prayer, particularly for children.

The prayer teaches that the source of all food is God, and that the food we eat is "God Blessed." This suggests that eating and living healthily are part of a blessed life.

The prayer also highlights the importance of the land of Sweden, invoking blessings on the country. It encourages a sense of national identity, pride, and honor.

Additionally, the prayer finally encourages a faith in the future, recognizing a God who eternal. It encourages gratitude for the big things in life as well as for the things we never thought would be possible.

Interestingly, the prayer also ties thankfulness to motherhood. Kids often associate thankfulness to the actions of their mothers.

Overall, the prayer teaches several lessons- about faith, national loyalty, health, and the recognition of God's role in the life of every child.

LESSON #1 – Learn the prayer.

LESSON #2 – Discuss why this is a good prayer for kids from any country.

THE POINT - The routine of thankfulness is a positive influence on both the child and the family. How?

Kids need to learn the power of a good influence on their life...

TABLE TIME PRAYER

God is great, God is good.
And we thank Him for this food.
And by His hand we all are fed'
Give us Lord our daily bread.

This prayer tells us of the true source of our daily food and provisions. It teaches us to be thankful and to recognize the true source of our blessings, in every form. It is a prayer of awareness. It is a prayer of gratefulness. It is a prayer of humility.

Though brief, this prayer hold great meaning for people of all ages.

LESSON #1 – Learn the prayer.

LESSON #2 – Discuss the meaning of the prayer.

THE POINT - Table time and table prayers are moments for teaching and learning.

Kids need to learn the history of prayers and prayers to God Himself...

> ### THE LORD'S PRAYER
>
> Our Father who art in heaven,
> hallowed be thy name.
> Thy kingdom come.
> Thy will be done
> on earth as it is in heaven.
> Give us this day our daily bread,
> and forgive us our trespasses,
> as we forgive those who trespass against us,
> and lead us not into temptation,
> but deliver us from evil.
> For thine is the kingdom and the power, and the glory,
> forever and ever.
> Amen.

The Lord's Prayer is probably the most frequently recited prayer in the world. Kids across the globe regularly recite this prayer, some even daily. It teaches us how to pray. It teaches the essence of prayer. Kids who learn this prayer have a model thay can follow throughout their lives. Often, this is where kids start their religious training. Parents would be wise to use this prayer in the home as a foundation for their child's spiritual development.

Consider this prayer as a condensed version of the Bible, all captures in about three minutes of reflection. It also serves as a way for children to connects with other kids around the world who are reciting the same prayer.

LESSON #1 – Learn the prayer.

LESSON #2 – Discuss the meaning of each phrase in the prayer.

THE POINT - Teach why it is good to learn from a Master.

Kids need to learn the meaning of "forever..."

> ## THE PSALM
>
> Glory be to the Father and to the Son,
> And to the Holy Spirit:
> As it was in the beginning, is now,
> And will be forever.
>
> Amen

Powerful lessons come often in short verses, such as this one. Though brief, but it teaches very important lessons about the Bible and the Trinity. It also is a main lesson on the eternal life span of the world.

LESSON #1 – Learn the prayer.

LESSON #2 – Discuss the meaning of each line in the prayer.

THE POINT - Small points can hold big lessons in life.

Kids need to learn the meaning of happiness . . .

> ### GOD, WHO HOLDS THE CHILDREN DEAR
>
> God who holds the children dear,
> Look after me, who is little
> Where ever in the world I wander
> My happiness is in God's hands
> Happiness come and happiness goes
> Thou remainest our Father.
> He who loveth God
> Obtaineth happiness.
>
> Amen.

A prayer of comfort and assurance. Kids grow and develop personal strength through the assurance of safety and love. As the prayer suggests love is the foundation of one's happiness. Without love, there can be no happiness. Parents are the primary messengers of love. Through them, kids come to understand what true happiness means.

It is also important to note that as a child comes to know and love God, happiness follows. It is the parent that teaches a child to love and to love God along with loving family and friends. The idea is to "smother" a child with love, so they learn to express love in return, starting with their family. This creates a beautiful circle of love, where love I both given and received. Happiness is the reward.

LESSON – #1 Learn the poem.

LESSON – #2 Discuss the meaning of the poem.

THE POINT - Ask if your kids if they feel safe and loved.

Kids need to learn to be thankful for the small things in life too . . .

A GOODNIGHT PRAYER

Thank you, God, for my cozy bed,
And the pillow for my head.
Thank You for my blanket too,
So, I can rest when the day is through.
I'll sleep until the morning light,
But now it's time to say goodnight.
Amen

Learning to give thanks is a fundamental lesson in relationship building. Being thankful, even for the little things, is vitally important. We develop an appreciation for the big and important things in life by first being thankful for the small things.

For children, things that may seem so small and insignificant to adults can be vitally important. What appears minor to an adult may be a big deal for kids. It is a matter of perspective. As adults, we need to see the world through the eyes of children. By doing so, we can truly come to understand and appreciate them.

LESSON #1 – Learn the prayer.

LESSON #2 – Discuss the meaning of the prayer.

THE POINT - Bedtime is a great time to learn how to connect and relate to others.

Kids need to experience a little fun at bedtime . . .

> ### GOOD NIGHT, MR. MOON
>
> Good night, Mr. Moon
> I'll have to go and leave you
>
> Good night Mr. Moon
> We will come back again and see you
>
> For while we're a sleep
> Through the window pane your're peeping
>
> We'll wake up and call out
> Goodnight Mr. Moon

A childhood prayer to the moon. Enjoyable. One way to help kids feel safe and protected while sleeping. It is one way to assure kids that they are not alone and that they are being watched over throughout the night.

LESSON #1 – Memorize the prayer.

LESSON #2 – Discuss the meaning of the prayer.

THE POINT - Bedtime can be fun and comforting time.

Kids need to learn how to be thankful for the small things in life . . .

THANK YOU GOD FOR THE GENTLE RAIN

Thank you, God, for the gentle rain,
That splashes on the window pane.
When mom says it's safe to go out for a while,
I jump and splash, and that makes me smile.

Being thankful is a skill that must be learned. We learn it by watching others, by writing a gratitude journal, and through determination and practice.

It is often the simple things in life, like a gentle rain, that teach us the basic lessons of life. Over time, we begin to connect these life lessons to a person, and that person is often our mother. Mothers are the primary teachers of life lessons. This prayer underscores that connection and give thanks to the mothers who teach us.

LESSON #1 – Memorize the prayer.

LESSON #2 – Discuss the meaning of the prayer.

THE POINT - Mothers are to be honored and loved.

Kids often need help in expressing gratitude to their family and friends...

GOD TEACH ME TO LOVE MY FAMILY AND FRIENDS

God, teach me to love my family and friends,
The way you love me.
You have love that never ends,
And that's the way I want to be.

This is a statement of understanding that love is learned. It also reminds us that it is possible to love endlessly. Of course, family and friends are the most important people in our lives, and our love for them is invaluable and worthy of being nurtured and learned.

The love of God serves as our model and guide. We often seek out role models we want to be like and become. The prayer is a way to ask for help in learning to love deeply, sincerely, and forever.

LESSON #1 – Learn the prayer from memory

LESSON #2 – Understand the meaning of the prayer for the child.

THE POIINT - Teach the value of having a model or guide in all areas of life.

Kids need daily encouragement to keep a focus . . .

A DAILY PRAYER FOR FOCUS

Dear God, guide my steps and direct my path
As I navigate through life's challenges.
Give me the wisdom to make sound
Decisions and the courage to follow my dreams.

Prayer is not just an exercise for bed time or meal time; it is something we can rely on daily. There are many things to pray for each day. Every day is stressful. Prayer helps us navigate the stresses of life. Each day goes much more smoothly when it begins and ends in prayer. We all need daily help and guidance, and prayer provides that support.

LESSON #1 – Memorize the prayer.

LESSON #2 – Understand the meaning of the prayer.

THE POINT - Any tough day or situation can be handles more smoothly with the help of prayer.

PART VII

Affirmations For Children

Affirmations are learned self-statements. Children primarily learn them from their parents, but also from teachers and family friends. After hearing such affirmations, kids begin to think of themselves in positive ways. They then begin to act accordingly, as well.

Fortunate are the kids who have been reared by parents and grandparents who speak positively to and about their children and grand-children. A solid foundation for self-esteem and confidence is thereby laid.

Self-esteem is acquired through affirmations and positive daily experiences. Unfortunately, many kids live a life without affirmations and statements of praise. As a result, they seek attention and a sense of importance though anti-social behavior or anti-social friendships, such as gangs. In many cases, they may also turn to deviant behaviors, such as drug use, to numb their feelings of hurt and loneliness.

Finally, affirmations are inexpensive means to rear a child and set a positive path for maturity and achievement. On the other hand, criticism and put-downs are costly means to rear a kid for a life of crime, failure, and loneliness. Parents make a critical choice as they determine how to rear their children and how they use affirmations in their daily interaction with their children.

Kids Need to ne Affirmed and Grow Because of it...

AFFIRMATIONS FOR CHILDREN

The Person I Am...

- I have many talents and abilities.
- I am valued.
- I am proud of my achievements.
- I am a good person
- I am loved and appreciated.

The Person I Am Becoming...

- I always try to do my best.
- I am a unique and special person.
- I am improving every day.
- I am doing better.
- I am going to make today count.

The Person I Am to Others...

- I am respectful and dependable
- I am appreciated for my kindness and compassion
- I am a good role-model for others.
- I am grateful for my family and friends.
- I am a good friend to others.

In the effectives use of affirmations, parents must first learn them and learn the lesson associated with each affirmation. Then they will be great teaching tools for any parent.

It's wise for parents to first learn the lessons behind the affirmation and then teach it to their children. Live out these affirmations daily in the home. Use them and teach them. Encourage the kids to use them with their peers.

LESSON #1 – Learn the affirmations so you can use them freely and often.

LESSON #2 – Reflect on and discuss the meaning of each affirmation.

THE POINT - Affirmations are mini-lessons in life. Use them often and wisely.

APPENDIX

Advice for Parents and Youth Leaders

Parents and youth leaders have a unique role in bridging the gap between a child and the music that influences them. Their role is to bring these two worlds together, helping children connect with the power of music. Singing instructs, encourages, and gives light unto a child's path. Here are some specific ways parents and youth leaders can be "people of influence" during critical times in a child's life:

- Help your child reflect on the basic lessons and underlying themes of the songs and choruses sung by children.
- Review the lyrics of the song and choruses with your child, sings and discuss the message of each song.
- Sing the songs and choruses with your child, enjoying the experience together.
- Reflect on and discuss the psychological lessons embedded in each song.
- Point out how a particular song or chorus can be helpful during the day for the child.
- Discuss how a particular song has been helpful to you during your growing years.
- Select a song and designate it as your "family song."
- Sing the family song often, discuss it, and repeat it frequently.
- Identify a few songs that you believe could be helpful for your child at any given time.
- Help your child understand why some songs are more helpful and why they should be sung repeatedly and memorized.

ALLAN G. HEDBERG, PH.D.

The Personal Impact of Music on Children

Throughout history, music has played a significant role in capturing and commemorating major historical event, providing us with both instruction and inspiration. For example, the birth of baby Jesus was marked by musical presentations and declarations. The praise at His birth, led by a choir of angels parading across the night sky, expressed adoration, and joy for Christ's arrival. This moment, celebrated through music, continues to resonate in tradiitons today.

Chants of celebration have been part of history – Biblical history, cultural history, social history, and anthropological history. Music records the history of people groups – their culture, life style, religion, and family life. The hallelujah chorus, for example, from Handel's Messiah welcomes Christ's presence and power. It is a symphony that has been honored and sung for centuries by young and old.

The same level of adoration and the use of music to promote celebration emotions, signify a significant historical event and marks the historical turning point throughout history such as the opening ceremony of the Olympics, the half-time of the Super Bowl, the coming home of soldiers from war and even hometown events on the 4th of July, Christmas, New Year's and Easter. Summer concerts on the lawns of the parks of America would be no exception.

So, what does this mean? Musical celebration and community events mark the path of history. However, the true importance is the message underneath such celebrations. The message and values conveyed by the songs and anthems selected to be played and sung on such occasions are long remembered. Yes, listen to the words. Listen to the message. Underneath the celebration and the celebratory events is the underlying message of American values and life. What is the message for every American? What is the message for every baby that experiences for the first time such celebrations in the parks of their city? This is the precise role of parents and youth leaders on such occasions. It is capturing the teaching moment and turning it into a lesson in life.

Perhaps the underlying messages of all of these events would be the price of freedom, the importance of honor, and value of hope. And don't forget, music instructs, encourages, supports, and heals. Make "teaching through music" a vital part of your family life and your youth program.

ALLAN G. HEDBERG, PH.D.

Competent Kids: Why Some Are and Some Are Not

In 2011, a research project conducted in Santa Barbara schools to evaluate the effects of songs and related activities on children's development and their social and emotional skills.

The study involved first and second-grade students from sixteen classrooms, with a total of 320 children participating. Each child listened to songs in a sequential order. College students were trained to provide forty-minute lessons using these songs and activities, held on nine Friday afternoons. Thelessons covered topics such as friendship and reaching out, respect and caring, celebrating differences, expressing and understanding feelings, and conflict resolution.

Significant changes occurred in both from listening to the songs alone and also by participating in school lessons. Some of the notable improvements in both first and second graders were as follows: increased confidence, following group rules, encouraging others to do their best, improved ability to approach peers, ability to use tools to stop teasing and bullying, understanding of the golden rule, resolving of conflict by talking out feelings, staying on task, positive attitude, and applying concepts learned from the songs sung in everyday situations.

Similar studies have shown that when time is devoted to the building of social and emotional skills, academic scores also improved. Despite historical tendencies for schools to prioritize academics through testing and drill, and minimize the use of music, these findings suggest that music-based learning can have a profound impact on overall development.

Many researchers have discovered that music activates neuro-systems of reward and emotions similar to those stimulated by food, sex, and drugs. Music has an almost magical ability to touch our souls and elicit strong healing responses. Music tickles the brain. Music releases endorphins that provide feelings of happiness and energy.

It is a fun way to make the medicine go down. Kids welcome tools to better handle their feelings, relationships, and practice positive thinking. Music is one powerful tool.

Anthropologists note that music is embraced by all cultures around the world in a variety of forms. It is the only thing people worldwide spend more money on than prescription drugs. Research also shows that music can strengthen learning processes, particularly by improved vocabulary and spatial-temporal reasoning. Music also has long-lasting effects for improved retaining of information. People often remember the song lyrics even if they haven't heard them for years. For example, some of the best examples of this is how most of us still recall the letters of the alphabet by singing the "A, B, C" song in our heads.

ALLAN G. HEDBERG, PH.D.

Books by Dr. Hedberg for Kids and Their Parents

- Doctor, Teach Me to Parent
- Better Parenting
- Kids Alive
- Psychotherapy Through a One-'Way Window

(All available on Amazon and your local bookstore)

Media Aps for Singing Kids

- MinistrySpark.com
- Truewaykids.com
- Hymnal.net
- Makingmusicfun.net
- Hymnary.org
- Ministry-to-children.com
- godtube.com
- whatchristianswanttoknow.com.
- archive.org
- songsforteaching.com

REFERENCES

Boni, Margaret. B., Fireside Book of Folk Songs, Simon and Schuster, 1947

C.D. Cedarmont Kids, Little David Presents, Action Bible Songs (17 Classic Christian Songs for Kids) produced by Mike and Sue Martin Gay

C.D. Cedarmont KIDS, Little David Presents, Sunday School Songs (15 Classic Christian Songs for Kids) produced by Mike and Sue Martin Gay

C.D. Cedarmont KIDS, Vol. 1 contains 34 songs!, 100 Sing-Along- Songs for kids, produced by Mike and Sue Martin Gay, Matt Huesmann and Chris Davis

C.D. Cedarmont KIDS, Vol. 2 contains 33 songs!, 100 Sing-Along- Songs for kids, produced by Mike and Sue Martin Gay, Matt Huesmann and Chris Davis

C.D. Cedarmont KIDS, Vol. 3 contains 33 songs!,100 Sing-Along- Songs for kids, produced by Mike and Sue Martin Gay, Matt Huesmann and Chris Davis

Lawrenz, M., *A Book of Prayers for Kids*, Wordway, 2018

Martin, *Cosmic Kids!*, Cosmic Kids.com, 2023

McGlothlin, B., *Praying for Boys*, Bethany House, 2014

Personal interviews with children's youth leaders, teachers, and parents

Scott, Kessa, *Sometimes, Means I Love You*, Amazon.Com, 2024

Tidal, *Kids Bible Songs*, Tidal.com, *2024*

www.ingramcontent.com/pod-product-compliance
Lightning Source LLC
LaVergne TN
LVHW061554070526
838199LV00077B/7045